CATCH
A
FALLING
ST★R

CATCH
A
FALLING
ST★R

a collection of poems and reflections

Charles Dan Worley

Word Wise Publishing, Inc.
Indianapolis, Indiana

Catch a Falling St★r

Permission requests can be sent to
Charles Dan Worley at charlesdanworley@yahoo.com

Facebook: @charlesdanworley
Website: www.charlesdanworley.com

Published in the United States by
Word Wise Publishing Inc.
Indianapolis, Indiana

All sketches by Charles Dan Worley
(Note: "Me and My Wagon" sketch was included in *Co-op: Coal, Community, & House 52* by Charles Dan Worley, June 30, 2020, Word Wise Publishing, Inc.)
Cover design by Wanda L. Worley

ISBN 978-1-952784-03-3 (pbk)
ISBN 978-1-952784-04-0 (hbk)
ISBN 978-1-952784-05-7 (ebook)

Dedication

With deep reverence, I dedicate this book to Mom. Without her encouragement at an early age, I may have gone a different direction. I can still hear her voice saying, "Danny, you can do and be whatever you want to be if you stay in school and get a good education."

What little talent I have, I attribute to Mom. She was so talented; she could look at a picture of a dress or shirt or pants in a catalog, buy the material she wanted to use, cut it out, and sew the pieces together. When she completed the piece of clothing, it looked as if it came from a department store. She could have been a clothes designer if she had lived in another time and place.

To Mom, Lexie Mae
4/5/21

Acknowledgements

Many thanks to my sister Gloria Ruberry and my nephew Leif Slusher for both taking the time to read and critique every poem in this collection. Their reaction I was able to compare to my feelings and intent as I was inspired to write.

To my sister Wanda L. Worley, who has poured hours into editing and in past days encouraged me to bring my poems to light, many thanks. Without her, this manifestation would not be possible and I would not have revealed my inner thoughts and a part of my personality for everyone to see.

Charles Dan Worley

Introduction

To assemble this many poems over several years, I owe a heavy debt of gratitude. When I wrote my first poem, I have to go to my college days at Cumberland College, renamed University of the Cumberlands in 2005.

In an English class under Dr. Frank Carnes, well into the semester, he had the class do a writing exercise. We were to read a short story from the perspective of our own experiences and feelings. We could not repeat anything we had read, only use it as a springboard to go in any direction we choose. It sounds easy, but it's very difficult, or at least it was for me. From this exercise of assembling words, I related it to a blank canvas before starting a painting: the beginning, the body of work, and the end. Writing triggered that same place of expression my art came from.

I write because I must, because when ideas or thoughts cross my mind to get them out they must be transferred to paper. Many I've lost through the years because when I was young without paper and pen available I'd tell myself I'll remember in the morning. When morning came, the words were long gone. My dream is that they will one day return and I'll have the good sense to write the inspiration down that very minute. That way I can return to it later. All those in this book are the ones I did not wait for a later time, but I wrote immediately as the inspiration came.

In the beginning as I tried to write, I kept those hidden for my eyes only to see. Occasionally, I would bring out one for my sister Wanda and her husband, Carlos Slusher, because at the time both were teachers. Their reaction was they could not believe I wrote the poem. This was the fuel I needed to continue.

While we are on this earth, the gift of learning is so important, and it's not complete until it's passed on. My sister Wanda has inspired me not to let the dust keep accumulating, but to reveal my poems for everyone to read. My hope is that at least one of my poems will inspire each reader to do something good for their friends or relatives. To communicate more and to express love more. We all can take small beginnings as we make this journey of life—we can make it better by effectively and continually learning to speak to each other. As we learn to speak, we will learn the dying art of listening to those around us.

My poems are pieces of who I am. Each one reveals why and what I was thinking about on a particular day. With premeditation and forethought, I've thrown open wide the doors to my inner sanctum. I don't expect to save humanity with this compilation, but I do hope what shines through is the power of love.

Love penetrates and wins with people who genuinely and honestly have a desire to communicate. Though I've left room for disagreement and it's okay, a hardy sharing of ideas on both sides. I dream that something between these covers will help you see your own self-worth, help you express your own feelings, or help you start your own path of creativity. If the love shared between these covers helps you strengthen a relationship, it would bring me much joy. If the human race can't be advanced by chipping away hate and negativity, then I will continue my search for a Falling Star.

Charles Dan Worley

4/5/21

Table of Contents

6. Looking Back: A Sundry Collection

7. Words of Love

8. Reflections on Religion

9. Denouement

To Catch a Falling Star

A beautiful innocent woman
Whose skin so fair and true,
Would I have to look near and far
Or would it be easier to try and catch a falling star?

Was there ever a time one could find
A beautiful woman so true?
Were they everywhere the wind blew?
If they were, those days are gone,
Could it have been a dream is where this woman lives on?

Was she and this youthful place for real
Could I find it before my hair turned gray?
I have to keep searching because deep within her
Beautiful is as an applique,
But if a woman such as this is found
I must know so that my search could end,
So that my heart could be renewed again.

I know, however, that by the time the circumstances
Of life permit me to encounter this paragon of a woman,
Will she be defiled
Or will she be just another woman?
So now, it will be more logical for me
To end this search for a true woman,
And instead to begin my search
For a falling star.

1972

1

A Collection

Between Beginning to End

A person's life melts like a whisper,
One can only get a glimpse of the person by
Listening to their words
Their thoughts are revealed.

No one can see the things they've done
Or what they've felt. A person's life is like the wind,
The sum total
Of where they've been is from beginning to end.

7/23/19
11:50 a.m.

The Full Moon

Moonlight through darkness
Still,
Restless in the wild can be heard even the
Whip-poor-will,
Sounds in the air are calling
Could it be love or is it a desire
For a brief moment,
Seems thrilling.

Unusually bright the moon through
Still air shines,
Restless lives stirring about mostly don't
Seem too fine,
But who can resist the tug and pull that
Words can't explain?
The gravity pulls harder at the innocent hearts and those
Alertly watching are the same.

But I wait seeking that which is sweet
And true,
The exhausting search sometimes leads to a
Rosy blue,
From the first moon beams to the flowery
Plucking blooms,
Who can deny the pain that turns into enticing
Sweet promise of the Full Moon?

9/17/20

The Pride of Man

The pride of man or woman
Some have many titles behind their name,
A woman with another woman thinks they've rose above
the man
Some countries stop educating girls at age eight,
They can't help thinking their minds are far superior
When in fact pride in the man blocks his smell,
He did not recognize the sweet aroma the woman wears
And the woman can't hear the kind words of the man di-
rected toward her,
Pride won't let them really see the other, each thinking
they're on top
Their minds will not let them see no two snowflakes are
the same

Or even two rain drops

Or

On a beach, even two grains of sand.
Who formed the nations?
No two leaves from a tree are the same
So as smart as you are, where were you at creation?

6/5/20

Mother's Day

The day once a year set aside
    To tell our mothers what we
Should have been telling them every day.

If there be some have ignored this day, let me remind you
    For all they've done,
We need a day to remind us what mothers do old and young
    If for nothing else, what about when we were young?

So, mothers, wherever you are
    Whether still close to touch or have moved on to a
    distant star,
The creator God passed on in you the bright of day
    And the twinkle of night.

The love he gave as he created the first man,
    The same love he gave to all mothers when you held
And nurtured all your babies, and my mother
    Watched me become a man.

1999

Who Can See the Wind?

The foreground is dark green
    The wind making the small ones move,
The background bright light green
    Can I see the wind when it moves?

Far above the mountain where they sit
    Moisture observes the blue,
Who can explain a bug as it lights?
    Days it tries still can't see the blue.

A pond with no escape sits perfectly still
    A stone without help sits alone,
When danger approached, my breathing slowed still
    A stone breaks from its place, falling, landing alone.

All these things move in and around
    Watching, studying the friction of the wind,
How can anything move without help or sound?
    Times I tried, who can see the wind?

7/5/19

Susie

Seeing her in a photo
Is what I base my analogy,
If not for a friend
She'd tell me where to go,
Critiquing someone I've never met I must take slow
Does she have a strong will, friendly and warm?
All these and more?
If I could sing, I'd sing her a song.
So, if I'm not trying to open a door
What is this good for?
Because I'm in awe of a beautiful face
What's behind it all,
I've heard a picture is worth a thousand words
Please allow me my thousand
Then I'll simply go walking barefoot in the sand.

Beneath Susie's facial structure
Is a woman confident of the what and where,
Her brain constantly working ever so sure
A word spoken slightly out of place sends to her brain an alert,
Beware, let it stay on the surface only in part
She smiles easily, that tells me she has a warm heart,
She'd never give anyone a second as she flashes her ring
Would she if I were a king?
She would not allow herself to look at a simple romantic.
On second thought, she might, and call me a maniac,
But she's too polite for that
The words coming through her lips with so much
understanding,

Lucky they are to be in her presence, of awe – standing
It's also inspiring,
It's too much for my brain to wrap itself around
If I stop abruptly, please know I'm having a shutdown,
This   is   Susie   to   look . . . AT.

8/21/19

Rainbow

I wish I could explain
    A rainbow after a rain,
How can the colors be explained
    The miracle after a rain?

Those have chased with empty hands
    It was real when they saw,
This half circle of bands
    The very spot it came to fall.

Maybe the other end, they thought
    Where the evidence could be,
Run and run as they sought
    Arriving it was not to be.

Invisible yet from the hands from above
    No one will ever catch or touch, only to see,
A rainbow is a promise from above
    I've seen it, my eyes I believe.

7/5/19

Without Fear

Centuries old the American Indians
    Way of life was strong
    For him it worked.
The air rippled with a twinge
    Of uneasiness over the horizon
    A new race was hard at work.

The trailblazer pioneers of a wilderness
    Come to know and love the life of freedom,
    The American Indian held sacred and would stand
    To the last man to die for.
The wind skims over the prairie centuries of
    Many moons seem to sweep past in a single night
    Changes were coming like they'd never known before.

Warriors from birth, adorned with feathers of eagles,
    Without fear they guided their way
    With their horse's mane.
Angry from many promises
    Earthly cares strong in their hearts,
    They looked down from the rocks
    And defined the plains.

Wave after wave they came
    Building shelters from trees,
    They called them houses
    Some were called forts.
Proud as he watched
    Hardly time to catch his breath,
    Could they know their time was short?

Redman he was called
    With respect, he was called Indian,
    As the moon hangs heavy on his wiki-up top
The last shot was fired.
    His memory survives through a state called Indiana
    That's all was given,
    Words of promises
    Vanished like the last dewdrop.

A melody wistful and haunting
    Disguised by sweeter the words were sung,
They were different
    Was that the cause to kill the old and the young?
The first peace treaty and after
    Food, peace, their own land,
    Washington knew the words were lies.
They lived a life of simple enchanting splendor
    Freedom as no other can come close to matching,
    Fairness and mercy they asked
    Can we hear their cries?

1984

The Question

If I could ever say it right
Or count the stars
    In the glimmer of your eyes,

If I could do what's right
To help you realize,
    Could you love me?

    Caring gives a woman peace of mind
Warmth of light inside,
    Raindrops of some dark night
    Would you love me?

Hearts have been broken
    Could love mend the hurt and revive,
And trust the feelings they believe
    Or fail thinking it's wrong when it's real?

Someday I hope you'll find that you love me.

If I could only do one thing
No one would hide to see,
    In your mind end the question
That makes you fall in love with me.

1991

Wedding Wish

When two are gathered
In his name,
From that day forward they'll
Never be the same.

They'll pledge their love
Till death do us part,
They'll say the words aloud
They've already said in their hearts.

They'll stand before God
And all the gathering,
They'll rise as one
And receive his blessing.

1992

My Youth

The gift of life is so wondrous
Vulnerable, innocent, completely dependent,
Acutely aware, yet mostly with our eyes closed
Feeling the breeze with wonderment,
As the bright stops hurting the retinas
Seeing the far gleams of a world that surrounds us,
When a butterfly scatters and the birds announce
Walking in the grass and beholds the bright,
Something suddenly is wrong
Nature perceives I will not harm it,
Enjoying the pleasures of the outdoors and the birds
Relax and sing a song.

Youth is waking up every day in a new world
Instincts become keen as growth continues,
The afternoon wind smells like rain and turns cool
But life impresses and lulls my thinking this could continue
on,
Suddenly the morning came of the first day of school
From one day to the next, expectations are to act like you're
all grown up,
Still continuing to grow, sometimes with tears
Tricked as though life was at a standstill seems,
Like a whirlwind the day came now looking back on my
teenage years
Even farther beyond to boyhood dreams.

Where did my youth go?
Knowing what I shouldn't and doing what I shouldn't
And did I waste my youth?
If possible, wouldn't it be better to postpone this wondrous
time?
It's better life isn't programmed that way
It might have been missed,
Remembering the only language youth understands
Is thrills and fun times,
The language of reason is impossible to understand
I also could have missed the Gospel Truth,
Wasted or not
I want to relive my youth.

5/2/20

Living Life

Living in harmony with nature
　　　What does it mean?
Do we simply excuse ourselves in a dream
　　　Or walking earth's beauty and see only the haze?

Life isn't an accident
　　　We are reminded each time we say grace.

Enjoy our days
　　　Looking for beauty that's worthy of our praise.

Never forgetting our position
　　　Then making a conscious decision,
Nature is a gift, savor it
　　　Manage it well, like you were handpicked to do it.

1993

Habit

Many spots around our lot
    Time weather-beaten and never replanted,
The rusty bottom fell from the pot
    From which the dirt was held now can't be planted,
The paint long since gone, the garage door looks sad
    Raising it up, it popped and cracked,
Being able to move if possible it seemed glad
    Now sitting alone, metal against metal raked,
She said, "I know it's a nasty habit.
    If I could quit, it would be divine."
She said, "It's like I'm a slave.
    Quit or not, we're going to die sometime."

Many years ago they had a brief encounter
    Fate decided their paths would once again to be,
Their eyes set on each other
    Two forces of nature move on uncertain with no
    guarantee,
Life's journey began, the years began to pile
    Leaving a man in a white coat, quit or die,
The habit now was strong, dismissing his words by denial
    Her blank stare forced only a siege,
She said, "I know it's a nasty habit.
    If I could quit, it would be divine."
"I have no willpower," she said,
    "Quit or not we're going to die sometime."

Getting up in the middle of the night
    It wasn't an outside sound, maybe it was her snoring,
While outside the sky slightly turning light
    Her habit was calling, burn just one before morning,
Go back her mind did say and try to sleep
    Only in sleep could she conquer the hold over her,
The warm covers slowed her mind not to speak
    Her middle-aged eyes close from the cold wind
    somewhere,
She said, "I know it's a nasty habit.
    If I could quit, it would be divine.
I cannot control the urge.
    Quit or not, we're going to die sometime."

Like months, the years swirled so many to spin
    Long last but like yesterday they stepped into old age,
Smoking all those years clustered together, she'd do it
again
    Living beyond those declared you won't see old age,
But still together after 45
    A full moon can stir the soul,
Forever the mind is young and alive
    Even though the body with many wrinkles has taken a
    toll,
She said, "I know it's a nasty habit.
    If I could quit, it would be divine.
It's too late, would it change anything?
    Quit or not, we're going to die sometime."

The days seem long it's an illusion
    Their days now filled with sitting on the swing and
    away from the ticking clock,
The swing chain was louder still, but it never got their
attention
    The birds skirted as they chirruped, one in particular
    on a rock,
What used to seem so far away
    Cherishing each moment knowing it could be any day,
Quit inhaling smoke was not an option now, no way
    There'll be time enough someday,
She said, "I know it's a nasty habit.
    If I could quit, it would be divine."
She said, "It would be redundant to try now.
    Quit or not, we are all going to die sometime."

11/29/19

Death of a King

Where did he go
That half only shown on TV
Shaking to the song hound dog and me?

See, see the rider on the mystery train
He left in a uniform on the day it rained,
Some thought he would never return, others knew
He would never forget his fans as he sang falling in love
with you.

From music to movies, he dazzled audiences in a flame
Star became stars in his chain,
They knew a few words with him
Would gain them fortune and fame.

Sun sessions to legendary performances all in one lifetime
Memphis to Vegas and the grass don't pay you no mind,
Can this really be happening as he shook and swayed?
He was just a poor boy and he did it his way.

His echoes of love sing on in our minds until we're gone
He will not be forgotten,
His words came through, I stumbled and I fell
All we have are memories pressed in the minds of us all.

Cades of laughter and songs, that's how I'll remember you
Memories that's all we have left,
His success penetrated the hearts of all
If you can only remember tears, then don't remember me
                    At all.

1977

Deserted House

It's worth the time
And inconvenience to seek a deserted house,
An old mining town is best
You might scare up a mouse.

Imagine the broken window panes
And the wide open doors,
The rotten front steps
The cracked walls and the filth-laden floors.

Let the spirit of these lonely
Deserted houses linger,
Day after day for years
Most just point their fingers.

Imagine how their Christmases
Must have been simple yet complete,
You might feel the agony of heartaches
Or the thrill of the joys if these walls could speak.

Imagine all you can
Until the gusting wind slams a broken shutter shut,
What once was a home but when it's abandoned
It decays into nothing more than a hut.

1973

Migration

Winter is on the move
Many restless nights I've seen
Though tonight is the night I break free.

High above the clouds I soar
Migrating by night, navigating by the moon and stars,
Been traveling far and fast
I'll continue my plight through day and night, I guess.

The compulsion that made me go
Was it the cold? I don't know.
Oh, where is home that I cannot see?
I hear echoes of voices, it must be she.

Flying over the land through sunshine and rain
Her signal is getting stronger pounding in my brain,
Many miles I've traveled
Many more ahead, though rest I seek,
I can't stop until tropical air warms my beak.

1976

Innocent Man

Someone who cares
Someone who dares
To listen.

Someone who dreams
Someone who seems
To miss me.

Someone who shares your affairs
Of tomorrow
Someone who sticks beside you through your joy and
sorrow.

I am an innocent man.

Some have accused me of being
A jealous guy,
My words you've taken wrong and
Later made you cry.

Someone who walks with you
In the sand,
Someone who doesn't
Care if you own a parcel of land.

I am an innocent man.

Projecting fingers, insensitive eyes
Watching,
Can they see my emotions or know
My love is wanting?

People say I'm thoughtless
And crazy,
Some have accused me of being mean
And have gone far enough to say
I'm a little bit lazy.

I am an innocent man.

1984

Retirement

When I was young, I heard of a time
When I wouldn't have to work,
Often in thought in my prime
It wouldn't last, mostly a quirk,
The thought of it I know I revealed a smirk
I heard others speak of that day
And how they couldn't save,
A boy thinks of finding his way
Thinking of a time nearing life's end is far, far away.

Most young couples don't realize
Parenting is only temporary,
Looking at others sometimes idolize
At my young age couldn't think that far ahead, nor
my contemporaries,
When the kids were young
Nobody ate until everyone sat down,
It was interesting from the oldest to the young
How their day went after it's done,
The young only think of finding their way
Life's end seems far, far away.

I remember all the homework
My son brought home from school,
When I got a job as a clerk
My responsibility was in tools
The long hours I could not help,

That which was brought home from school
It proved to take all his heart,
Young adults think only of finding their way
The end is pushed into the future far, far away.

Sleep was not possible
Until I heard the lock turn on the door,
A son thinks he is capable
Of managing his own way and more,
Suddenly realizing parental authority
Is all but used up,
A young son evokes his priority
Let me grow up,
A son's will is his way
What used to be, now isn't far away.

All of a sudden the word retirement
Is being used a lot,
Reviewing my financial statement
I said out loud, "This will be my lot."
This was the path I chose, I couldn't feel resentment
Never thought I'd make it,
Without delay the day arrived
Money and the lack of it,
It flutters the heart repeating deprived
My devotions to my family was the way
Now's the day I can't push away.

I look back on the day
The day I once dreaded,
With all the time, no money to buy
Things I once thought important I now discarded,
All life's struggles, desired emotions will collide with hope
Waking up with nothing to do,
The worrier will not be able to cope
Again it comes down to your mate and you,
Managing daily medicines graduated to a full-time job
Weather has beaten my car rough as a cob,
Are you spending endless hours complaining?
The love of life is faith, love, hope,
Where's your focus?
My mind will wonder on the days that were now on us.

Thinking of days gone by and the joy that was there
Be thankful when life was so complicated I found support,
Finding something I love from days that were
Or else retirement could be short,
I'm busier now than when working a 40-hour week
I've solved the question too much time on my hands,
A balance of life now I seek
My days are filled with things I love,
While the world is constantly working toward modernity
Retirement is next door to eternity.

4/12/20

Sounds Made in the Dark

Thunderstorms, lightning briefly
    Brighten with light,
Far away a coyote howls waking up
    The others that sleep through the night.

Earth tremors ripple through
    Some parts of the world,
Pressure cannot be overcome, though one tried
    In the city streets with the help of a girl.

Winter came
    Outside the snowflakes gently falling,
Some nights
    Are restless and he dreamed of something.

Restless he lay awake
    Nervous about all the years gone by,
A woman lying in his arms
    Wondering her thoughts but couldn't see her eyes.

I love you words
    Whispered in the dark,
In a love affair
    Promises aren't made from the heart.

Slowly, ever so slowly the air timeless
    Pressed in the morning light,
The sun shimmering brightness
    Pushes out your thoughts of the previous night.

Storm systems, earthquakes, pressures that build
    Mountains and volcanoes then pull apart,
As sure as the earth rotates and the moon continues to
shine
    There will be sounds made in the dark.

1984

Turning Point

I'm concerned and sometimes worry about
   My country.
   When groups only yell and will not listen
   To others they disagree.

Is my love for this country enough when I
   See those with clubs destroying
   Property of others their hate cannot compensate?
   Will truth once again be our guide and not twist
   And pervert to credit the sides?

As a people, have we forgotten history or ignore
   It by sticking our heads in the sand, tearing
   Down a monument of stone? Is your feeling that
   Fragile? Did it go away? Is it fair to apply
   Standards of today to those of yesterday if
   Rewriting what really changes history?

There were those I'm sure never thought Rome
   Would fall but did it? Was it the forces
   From within? They were blinded by their own
   Immorality, whatever they wanted to do, and
   If it felt good they did it, that's ok,
   It became their reality.

The world would love it if we the country should
   Fail and fall. We've been infused with the
   World's pain bringing to the surface group
   Against group. Is the result of it taken in vain?
   Will we rise above and harass the insane?

Is our reality a false reality? Is the thread that
   Holds what we know so fine that the
   Fail safe certainty, insecurities, and systematic
   Relativity could break? Could we come back
   From the brink or would we vanish into
   The dust pan of history like Rome?
   Still even then would the survivors stick
   Their fists in the air and say we are proud,
   We did it on our own?

8/21/19

The Crown

In the year two thousand nineteen, who was
    talking about a chip?
A microscopic thing designed for under the skin
Digital certificate for health reasons was the purpose for
the chip,
Is this what's spoken of at the time of the end?
More than ever this is the time for those talented to play
the guitar
A small circle of light of the sun seen around,
It's long straight sided of the shape of a cigar
Where is the crown?

Wuhan was getting support from America studying
    virus in bats
Back and forth she came collecting support,
Off to China with money in their hat
Their superiors euphoric seeing the report,
It's still unclear the beginning
Naming it the China virus, we're called racist,
Did a bat get loose unknowing?
China lied about the number of initial cases
Is this the seat of the crown?

The rarefied gases envelop the sun
An irregular pearly glow around the moon,
Light reflecting colors on the corona around the sun
Only then can it be seen around the darkened disk of the
moon,
The country from shore to shore closed down
Cruise ships impacted by the coronavirus,
Airplanes sitting quietly without a sound
Stock market down with high losses,
Could it be healing started in the ozone around?
Who can pinpoint the crown?

While the opposition were trying to impeach
They opposed on every hand,
The Chinese said it was contained there wouldn't be any
outreach
They lied about the activity in Wuhan,
The president instituted a travel ban
Immediately he was called a racist,
January 2020 stopped those wanting to land
Their claims proved there was no basis,
Unemployment reached an all-time high
New guidelines ordered, stay home don't go around,
Avoid touching just say bye
No alternative the economy shuts down,
Wash often with soap and water
Was this the purpose of the crown?
People in general were afraid and tense
Staying apart might protect your daughters,
Use a germ killer regularly
Go out only if absolutely necessary,

Avoid crowds regularly
Do your part it's absolutely necessary.

China will not let people go into Wuhan
But people from there go all over the world,
A good substitute would be vital
As they traveled the disease spreading all over the world,
The restrictions got worse yet it was okay to go to Walmart
Can't stop helping China and a man named Bloomberg,
I'd rather stay home and throw darts
Helping a billionaire isn't attractive even if Walmart
is in Williamsburg,
Was this a way to bring the masses around?
Which one has the crown?

From birth I've always heard
Get out, get your exercise, run and play,
Now like animals we're being herded
Being told to stay inside, stay away
Even people appear to be healthy,
I'd rather sit outside and watch the birds lurch
How can people sitting on the couch stay healthy?
Government ordering people don't go to church
Quietly hoping people will run and tell,
When looking at the surface of it all it's clear it has a
smell
Name it what you will, the Chinese, the Wuhan, or even
corona,
Are they subverting?
Who has the crown?

4/6/20

Don't judge me by what

I say,

See me, the good that cannot

Be spoken.

1984

2

All in Fun

Pants or Shorts

Sometime ago I was on the porch at my brother's house
We were resting from a day without our wives,
The quiet was as serene as a church mouse
We realized the dullness without them would be our lives.

What happens then is like a story being reborn
Suddenly his neighbor returns we know not from where,
Stopping in front of his house he toots the horn
We knew not the urgency and not yet ready to leave our
chairs.

Opening his door, he yelled, "Come out here and get this
s---."
Without delay the wife went walking to the car,
Some I know will say this is not legit
Don't excuse it by saying I had one too many at the bar.

The wife appeared carrying two very large drinks
We thought the man would be burdened with bundles of
stuff,
We gazed and gazed without even to think
Surely the man had more than enough.

Then my heart delighted when the man appeared
He, too, was burdened with only one small bag,
A long moment ensued before we openly cheered
How could this man not later brag?

My heart with pleasure fills with chants
Could it be the man was in a hurry to watch sports?
My brother and I determined this man wears the pants
Even though at the time the man was wearing shorts.

10/5/19

Facilities

Who can resist the pain of the body?
Would you say no to a building?
Relieved of the pain, how good you feel in your body
The opposite is exposing.

There are some would not go in
Those who think they are better than they,
Many have, you would not call friend
For years it was the way.

If you go behind a rock or tree
Who are you hiding from?
Only a small area those cannot see
They think they are completely hiding,
                    Even though from some.

To like someone by your standards might be conceited
Don't call someone you know nothing about a louse,
It was a welcome site only when it was needed
Once upon a time there was one by every house.

7/10/19

Outside Toilet

It was nonexistent until the time came to go in
Was never a pleasant sight,
How soon you followed or how long it's been
No matter the weather or time of night.

Is closet a better word?
Opening the door, out a wasp flew,
Only crickets yelling I heard
It was hard getting used to.

Suddenly without warning you and the building went for a
ride
Bad luck getting caught in on Halloween night,
Not me, I wanted to hide
Who's responsible for this headache on Halloween night?

Which neighbors you think it be
A calculated guess next year you'd turn one over too,
Would you try and repay those that did the deed?
Can you forgive if it happened to you?

7/25/19
8:52 a.m.

Can't Hold Back

Enjoying some quiet time before the big day
We made ready all the cleaning was over,
Also going the two couples came the same day
Everything was done as we remember.

Enjoying each other's company and all the news from
whence
The medical problems of one and the issues of that,
What one person's able to endure sometimes it's only a
glimpse
Or if knowing would ask the question he alone could do
that.

As the one laughed at his bowels and the horridness it
brings
The telling was so hilarious we, too, laughed with him,
Scratched his head as he told everything
But still we were drawn into his story as we looked at him.

Travelling is difficult not finding a john quick enough
Who can hold back the forces of nature when it's time?
The bustling highways can be rough
It's never easy when you can't hold back needing more
time.

Finally stopping found a place
We all thought his troubles were over,
The weary travelers on the road kept moving to their place
Hurry, his mind kept repeating over and over.

Almost running, inside he found the men's room
Relief he knew was his as he relaxed,
To his surprise the door was locked and there he stood
What he always feared had maxed.

Under his breath knowing it wouldn't help, he begged
Like a statue staring at the door,
A warm feeling now running down his leg
His leg became a highway as defecation puddled on the
floor.

Now he prayed for the door not to open
Not touching the eyes of anyone or anything to say,
He felt trapped as in a pen
His only option, he simply walked away.

10/3/19

When I was younger

I felt I could

Move the earth.

Now I feel the earth moving beneath me.

1984

3

That Western Feel

He Rode On

He rode alone
Trail dust separated into miniature rivers,
Time forgot the last breeze blown
Sweat beads unafraid like high mountain divers.

In the path ahead could be rest, maybe danger
Saddle sores without warning began aching,
Human company welcomed, his hand gripped cold steel
Similar images flashed his memory overtaken.

Animal instinct seeing the same could not comprehend
Silence remembered, favored above a pounding hoof,
Leather beneath, breath expelled into the wind
Both were one standing a hill above.

Restlessness nature could not harness
Quietly the shade lifted his eyes to see,
The miles behind changed to deep bone weariness
Curious eyes wondering the same as he.

The sun set now in its place
Weather beaten skin hid the secrets he'd become,
A thought lingered of her many a caress
He rode on.

1994

Cowboy

High lonesome sounds
  Whether riding drag or singing to steady the cows
  Maybe drifting through any old town.

Friendly to those would receive it
  Ready as a lion to anyone being coy
  Please, my name's not Rory.

The only important things in his life
  His horse, saddle, hat, and gun
  These sustained his life.
  The thought stayed in the back of his mind
  Like a proud feeling a father gets thinking of his son.

Pleasure came many ways
  One in particular after a long day,
  His rough dried parched fingers strumming his guitar
  With gentle tenderness that would settle the roughest
  beast,
  Seemingly the night, the stars, and all of heaven
  Was enjoying the sound he made,
  As if in a concert hall
  Only the cows his audience and the heavens his judge,
  He accomplished his purpose
  The herd so quiet not making a sound,
  As their hoofs tomorrow pounding the ground
  Their strength they'd draw on now.

The air he breathed was rich with moisture and fresh
    Back in the saddle early hardly any rest
    Burning daylight could not get passed,
    The steely eyes so keen
    Couldn't remember the last time he'd seen anything
    green,
    Hoping for another day without incident
    Not knowing what lurks in a ravine
    Or hiding around a bend,
    Content to let the day play out
    Energy would be wasted on what could be about,
    Reminding himself what he was doing
    His horse beneath him in the wide open spaces,
    Pushing them little doggies through
    The simple country far and wide
    Loving his work and if possible took his breath and
    sighed.

Up ahead the chuck wagon and campfire in view
    Another day almost through,
    A few hours rest and tomorrow he'd do it all over again,
    Dang it, he said, no,
    My name's not Rory,
    That's why they call him a Cowboy.

8/22/19

Blue Boy

It was raining when he left
He was too young to leave, he thought as he rode,
It would be hours before he slept
Had to keep following the tracks of his son's horse before
they ran cold.

Thieves he hated, the rain now beating harder
They'd never been this close to getting away,
Shelter he has to find as it keeps getting darker
Under a rock ledge, so tired as he thought if possible he'd
make them pay.

First light he searched, no tracks he found
His son's heart would break knowing his horse was gone,
Bad luck it was only nature making a sound
His son would see him in the distance he was riding in
alone.

Ranch life was hard, harder for a boy losing everything he
owned
Almost home couldn't believe is that his boy running to
meet him,
Stepping off his horse, his boy jumped in his arms.
He came home, Pa, he came home.
You mean Blue Boy came home? He's in the barn, Pa; let's
go see him.

7/7/19

Call Me a Cowboy

Sunlight has barely tilted through the windows
Already he's awake and dressed,
Horse hooves echo over the smell of bacon
In the saddle he rests.

April in Texas harvest time
The main chore to be done,
She stood in the doorway
As he rode on under the rising sun.

Harsh realities of rangeland that offered nothing but
misery
Yet without a semblance of complaint,
For he lived by the code and the harsh body punishing job
Could not dim the image he would forever implant.

Then came the herds
Pushed over scarcely fragmented plains for miles,
Like drill sergeants the others followed
Through rivers, gullies, and the wilds.

From a low voiced word
Night watch began through sleepy eyes,
Looking upward to the glittering stars
In the now clear sky.

High lonesome songs filled the air
To untighten the cattle's nerves,
The old Chisholm Trail lullabies
Ever so softly could be heard.

Far off he wandered
Until the daylight came on,
Wanting no more than a shot of rye
A hot meal and a woman alone.

When the sun shines brightly
His mind will be clear again,
Overworked and dirty all in a day's work
It's almost time to turn in.

Sleep came easy
When the night watch was over,
His saddle now his pillow
A dusty old quilt for cover.

Young America it was a land of sweeping grandeur
As he sat on a hill overlooking its edge,
Steely gaze a heartbeat strong captured a particular time
and place
Range life manifested inside his head.

Bigger than life riding the wind of endless miles
In truth hardly a boy,
Reality overshadowed by hard riding and fast shooting
A seed of heroic legend, I guess that's why they
                                    Call me a Cowboy.

                                    1984

We'll look back on our lives

Time and again,

We'll dance again,

We'll sing again,

We'll laugh again,

But

We'll never be young again.

1980

4

Looking Back: Co-operative (Home)

Where Are My Wages?

When am I being paid?
I was paid company script, no money
    As I asked for more,
That's all you're getting, the man said.
Is this for real I could only spend
    It at the Company Store?

The rent is due
    My TV payment is too,
Everywhere it's the same "No"
    Can't borrow more,
It's good I don't own a car
    The man said he'd sue,
Hard to get ahead when my
    Wages go first to the Company Store.

The electricity was cut off, lost my
    TV to the service man,
All I have is my family like the
    Birds that soar,
No delays my wages came on time
    All smiles when I saw the man,
We still get to eat, take what you want
    My pockets empty again as I walked
        From the Company Store.

7/23/19
1:57 p.m.

Dad

Weekend Dad

Mom made herself many a blouse
Out of flour sacks when moved to a blue house,
Waiting on worktime to start
A five-minute walk to the Company Store,
I could not forget my first pop was bought there
A favorite place sometimes to gather,
Walking up the hill to the mantrip, every man
With pick and shovel in hand,
After loading, a ten-minute ride to the face
The powder and shot mixed with coal dust heavy to taste,
My dad's headache came soon after
Smiling that Worley smile no one knew the pain he was
under.

Every morning as long as could remember going under
earth and soil
Backbreaking jobs digging for coal,
Carrying tools he needed and convinced himself he was
ready
Reading his place his carbide lamp also ready,
Without warning the next morning work was shut down
No money saved and little to nothing owned,
No way to travel, where to start
Like a harpoon piercing his heart,
So many questions, how would his family last
The least of which was covering his baby's feet,

Overwhelmed with what would he do and nowhere to
look
Or no mood to go throw a hook,
Day after day goes by with no prospects
Also suffering was the family pet.

Seemingly there was no way out
All eyes were on Dad to be the one without doubt,
The pressure of doing something was no little thing
It seemed the strongest every morning,
What would he do echoing the loudest sound
Drinking coffee from used coffee grounds,
The kids were crying, starvation was gathering at the door
An unexpected knock came to the front door,
The man at the door was seen before
He came with a good report,
You can find work you'll have to leave
Spirits were lifted yet hard to believe,
Overnight the rising sun shown on our clad
Daddy became a weekend Dad.

5/30/20

Me and My Wagon

Me and my wagon
When I saw it the first time,
The power it offered
And knowing it was mine.

The first thing I did was sit on it
After to the top of a hill I pulled it,
Raised my feet off the ground and I was gone
Me and my wagon.

My friend and my passion
Me and my wagon,
When I was seven
The gift of youth so wondrous has to be from
heaven.

It opened up new places of going
Instead of always running,
Sometimes I could ride
Instead of always carrying,
It was more fun pulling
Me and my wagon.

It elevated me to transportation
Hauling to new expectation,
Many new ways
A new way transporting gallon or gallons
For me and my wagon.

It was hard for grownups to see
The added fun it offered knowing it was behind me,
Ignoring the buzzing of a flying dragon
Now the importance of me and my wagon.

My old friend went where I did
I pulled my wagon up the dirt road barefooted,
Crossing the creek picking the rocks
I stepped on hoping I was surefooted.

By now my old friend has been replaced
When I was eleven,
It was as good maybe better I reckon
Me and my wagon.

My wagon was not store bought
But that which came from a tree sought,
Scavenging through forest bush
The wood fitly jointed but not rushed,
As Mom's radio played a song
Me and my wagon happened along.

Often I imagine would I go back there
To me and my wagon,
By the heavens
For none is higher to swear,
And swear I would
As fast as a minute
I'd be riding the air.

5/28/20

Rayma Dean

Now's the time long ago
Sitting in the classroom ahead of me enough I could see,
A young girl so pretty I'd like to get to know
Her name was Rayma Dean,
And this girl gave no thought
To someone like me.

She was young and I was young
On this playground I could see,
She would not give me the look of love the look I knew
The heavenly eyes of Rayma Dean,
Patiently I waited but the glow in her eyes
Never came to me.

We grew to young adults
Separated still further so far my eyes could not see,
The wind was not responsible but who can say
Was it the changing tide that overshadowed Rayma Dean?
Whatever the words, the words spoken over her
It was not the words from me,
She's so far away my eyes will never again
Come down on her to see.

When we were younger if she had gave me something
Something just for me,
When we saw each other one time after many years
The olive branch she held, my eyes should have been more keen,
It could be me saying that's my Rayma Dean

Wondering what could've, what might have,
Nor angels, nor stars blinking at me
Can keep my mind from thinking
I met the beautiful Rayma Dean.

Those older and wiser might say
I stumbled, time rolled over me,
The chance was so slim when it came I could not see
I missed my chance with Rayma Dean,
How I long for eventide when I lie down to sleep
She may wave at me from some distant cloud,
You can see me the next time you dream
Dreams come and go without whispering a sound,
A thought like lightning came to mind
I will see you again,
No doubt it was her
The beautiful Rayma Dean.

8/9/19

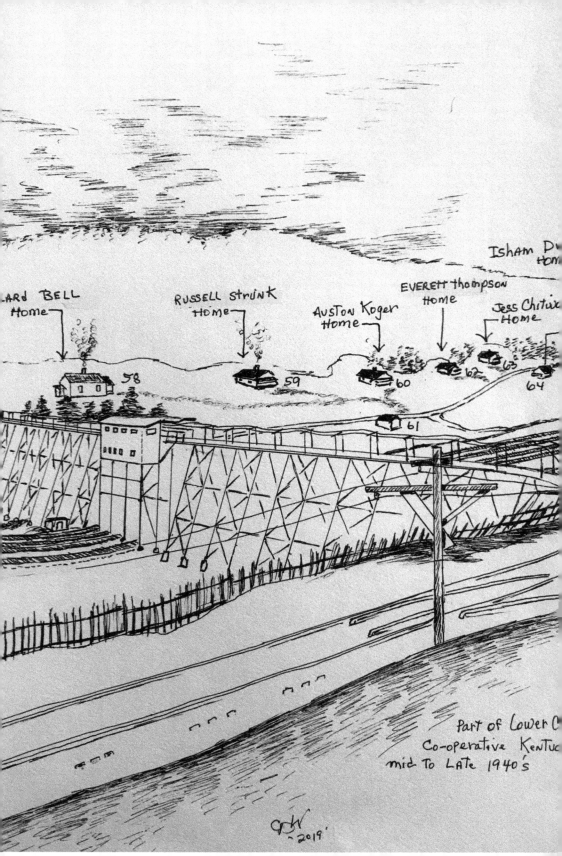

Isham D[...]
Hom[...]

[...]ARd BELL
Home

RUSSELL STRUNK
Home

EVERETT thompson
Home

AuSTON KoGer
Home

Jess Chitu[...]
Home

58

59

60

62

63

64

61

Part of Lower C[...]
Co-operative Kentuc[...]
mid To Late 1940's

2019

The Co-op Tipple

There once was a place
That still holds my heart and mind,
A structure resembles a web standing there
The dust from it caused by the nearby coal mine.

The structure stood high and long
It cradled those no matter how many,
Never complained of all it had to do
One thing could be said it didn't shine like a new penny.

Travelers are greeted because of the enormity from east to
west
The morning sun can't help reflecting,
On the other side casting a shadow from cliff to cliff
The evening sun cools down after all-day adoring.

Anyone leaving they will say
It always beckons me back,
Can't wait to return it always seems to smile
Did you miss me? So glad you came back.

Would you believe those Kentucky hills I call home
Each time I stood close I felt so little,
The old town lives on in my mind
The structure was just the Co-op Tipple.

9/12/20

Moments I've Lived

Glimpses of the life ahead
Shown as I lay in my bed,
Understanding was far away
The race I'm in is appointed this way,
Or no concept of day and night
Even flashes of bright celestial light,
Finally dimmed more frequent through opening my eyes
The mysteries of our lives,
Beneath me spun hours, weeks, years
Every life experiences rain and tears,
Walking, running, and playing
Under her commands obeying,
My steps guided by the watchful eyes of Mom
Through weeds of knowledge on my own,
Happy those early days I was
Joy builds me up as it does,
My hometown was built with mountains all around
Mostly barefooted those kids made the sweetest sound,
A creek meandered all the way through
Houses lined the hills where spring water drew,
In the foreground stood a web of wood and steel, a tipple
After the spring rains the creek rushing created a ripple.
It spanned from cliff to cliff
For years it proved enough,
In the middle was place for playing ball
When work stopped nothing could stop the fall,
Living by oil lamps for light
Frightening cat screams in the night,
Work or studies we made it through

In me knowledge grew,
Materialism wasn't the driving force
Love, hope, and food was our daily course,
It wasn't shameful to walk to family and friends
Looking at the sky and back down again,
Every life is important not because of things
But the lack of things no door bells to ring,
We lived a more simple time
A lot of money for a kid was a dime,
We didn't have 24-hour news
Now, 1000 times a day until it's used,
How we lived is important to remember
A potbelly stove in the corner,
Eat or heat came from burning
Wood or coal was best when turning,
We accomplished so much with so little
Now we have so much no time to whittle,
The scent of honeysuckle faintly coming and going
Daffodils barely rising above the grass adoring,
Other kids now heading to class
Saturday afternoons fishing for bass,
Hearing the school bell rang
Occasionally Rayma Dean sang,
Walking down the dusty road barefooted
A car passing by tooted,
Click and wheel Charles himself might chase
Inside the Company Store staring into a narrow case,
Going home with peanuts and a pop in hand
The airways played different bands,
It was a time without devices of communication

Quiet time wasn't bombarded with confusion,
Who doesn't want time to slow down
Their actions make empty sounds,
60 years ago no computers or phones
A trusty wagon was the sum total I owned,
Quiet serenity I'm so blessed to have lived through it
Growing so fast hard to have clothes to fit,
Hearing the sounds of home still adoring
As a kid around the breakfast table captures this
Moment I'm living.

3/27/20

Learn Before You Can Go

Often I wish I could go back, way back when,
When I was a boy wanting to go swimming with the boys.
The boys said, "We're going, you coming along?"
Along the way somebody said, "Where you boys head-
ing?"
"Heading," they all said at the same time, "Swimming is
where we're going."
"We're going on, you come when you can."
"Can I go?" I said again, "The boys are getting restless."
"Restless changed, we're going, you meet up with us later."
"Later I will, is it still the blue hole?"
"The blue hole!" The voice of authority said,"That's too
deep."
"Too deep?" The boys said, "It's perfect for swimming."
The commanding voice said again, "You have to learn
                    How to swim before you can go."

7/8/19

CO-OPERATIVE, KENTUCKY

HOUSE 52

GWORLEY
3-10-20

Not Being Seen

One day I was walking home
I'd been catching minnows on my own,
For sure by tomorrow I'd know if it passed the test
The creek by the Co-op school seemed best,
Walking down the dusty road barefooted
Hearing voices in the distance I froze there looking,
I stopped before I was seen
I was taken by surprised, how could this be?
The main camp was beginning to come into view
The voices I thought I heard it's true,
Peeping through the trees to the porch of the house
It was the same kids I met last summer at this same house,
Of which was the prettiest girl
By her presence alone was able to change my world,
My mind would get all mixed up and I couldn't speak
Could I let her see me in my bare feet?
If I left the cover of the trees
I would be spotted for sure in the open breeze,
Here I decided to wait
The power that held me was my own character flaw I hate,
By the road off to the right
A grassy area I sat down in the quiet,
I wondered how long when they'd leave the porch
Over at the Company Store another food transport,
This wasn't the right time to show myself
I had to wait it out forcing myself,
Now I had time to reflect with no hindrance

Time occupied thought was of the utmost importance,
Three boys and a girl came to visit a neighbor for a week
Playing with the boys I had no trouble finding words to
speak,
Only around the girl my utterance I could barely under-
stand
In the juvenescence it's different and I haven't held her
hand,
I shouldn't let what others think or don't see
So here I am can't move on by my own inadequacies,
But ridicule and laughter I could not take
I didn't want to even give the slightest to make,
Staring at the open space I had to cover
Seemed like hours had passed as I searched for another,
They were visiting one of several houses in a row
Would it be any better if their arrival was tomorrow?
My hoping they'd go inside was not to be
I had to have a new plan to not be seen,
I decided to cross on the walk bridge
The main road was before the ridge,
It provided more cover to not be seen
Knowing it would be worse if I was caught in this scene,
So across the bridge I ran
Getting out of this trap and,
Moving felt free and
Getting home I'd contend for the upper hand,
On the far side of the store building I made it that far
Lucky for me down the dusty road didn't come a car,
Only a few steps to a partial block building
The distance was expanding from my beseeching,

Only thing was it would be directly in line with anyone
paying attention
One more open space where the road came to the crossing,
As I ran crossing the space couldn't help thinking what a
day it'd been
The only thing I can point to, I succeeded at not being seen.

3/31/20

Jewell

Behind the face of Jewell was the face of strength
She never wavered from life's hard blows
Pieces of oak split and cut the right length
Raising her children alone, though.
Is a combination of a woman's resolve character and worth
I can see the gentle face of Jewell
Her trained eyes also gave warmth
Concerned for others was a natural rule.
In her prominent position she was always down-to-earth
Myself it's inexcusable how can I get past
Where was I, her last years on earth?
If seeing her would I have been the last?
Every day sitting in her chair looking out her door
Though she's gone I've revisited her store,
Empty, her store still looks the same
My sadness overwhelms me just speaking her name…
                                                    Jewell.

So different from a shiny single stone
Rushing creek over rocks looking like foam,
So you see it's ok to call me a dunce
What's important now should have been then,
All these pieces of regret coming at me at once
If I had listened and embraced it way back when,
Today regret would not be trying to beat me to a mound.
Staring and standing and looking around
Is it something somebody found?
Jewell's place was more than a place to buy food

A gathering place finding out the news and the happenings
Talking, enjoying the company around the potbelly stove
too,
The timber mixed with coal crackling
Somebody said better go home see what mama's got
cooking,
No one was in any hurry to start
There's more coffee Jewell said before you depart.

Knowing I could have seen her as often as everyday
How could I let life get in the way?
This I live with everyday
Hope one day we'll see each other again
Her forgiving eyes will see me still as friend.
Until then my thoughts are as yet
The price I pay now for regret,
Her chair quietly in its place sits still
No one stops on their way over the hill,
Or the floor doesn't ripple from a stranger named Lil
Where are the voices respected no cussing was the rule,
There was a time feed for your mule
How fast it goes no one explains the chill,
Or two old men trading knives and making a deal
Why do things have to change?
Our seemingly complicated lives we try to rearrange.
By the time we realize it's too late
The control our simple sharp minds face the mistake,
Finally we give into a wonderful place in time
Standing in the very place likened to a hint of divine,
It stirred me to how far and wide I failed Jewell
Recalling of a simpler life,

So rich the story of Jewell is also the story of mine
That's why it takes my breath away thinking of her,
Beneath our lives so picturesque so intertwined.
Her voice in my ear so near
Jewell...Jewell...Jewell
In my breath your days, your life mingled in a
                        Heartfelt breeze as I speak
                                    Jewell.

8/21/19

Hickory Knob

Walking a path through a rich forest
The forest was prime virgin timber,
At the end of the path
It opened up to quiet serenity.
Is this the Knob?

I asked those I met
The answer was the same,
I searched but couldn't find
This place called the Knob.

Sunday afternoons waiting on church time
Playing horseshoe games,
Taking time out to eat chicken 'n dumplings
The few farms I saw taking a day of rest,
Kids laughed when I asked, "Where's the Knob?"

I found a lot of shucked corn cobs
Hard work and raising their own food,
A barn two mules standing eating hay
But where is the Knob?

It was a part of heaven
Isolated from the rest of the world,
A lot of hickory nut trees
Everywhere I turned I felt peaceful,
I'm now thinking there may not be a Knob.

Could this be only felt in the heart?
Trees so full an occasional apple hits the ground
One room church made from logs,
I finally found what others already knew
On top of the mountain looking around,
The Knob isn't a knob at all.

8/9/19

Dreams I've Lived

There's never any doubt
This place I grew up and went about,
Who could have forsook
The changing years it took,
It was never known to me
My world would not always be,
I grew up happy as could be
What changed who said this was not to be?
I didn't know my education was formal
I went about the days as normal,
It was the best of times for a child
Playing and running wild,
A hole in my shoe sole by school year's end
Setting those things aside like an old friend,
Every year it was the same
Couldn't wait to go barefoot in the rain,
Sleeping long the mornings away
There'll still be time to play away the day.

Oh, simple life there back in the day
Hearing kids laughter far away,
It's my story of the early days
Our days were full of things to play,
Mom made visitors welcome to our home
Sitting on the porch she'd sing us a song,
Gnats and mosquitoes tried attacking around an oak
They couldn't withstand an ole rag smoldering smoke,
Mom made most of our clothes on her Singer
Some might call our existence meager,

Better not say that out loud mister
You might get one across the keister,
We played together with so much fun
No thought given to the heat or sun,
Let's play 'board on deck' somebody said
Smelling sweet Mom-made gingerbread,
What about marbles everybody can play
Be careful losing too fast could be a short day,
Knowing I lived through a time people today only dream
of
I revisit often those times I love.

Can you imagine without computer or a phone
Or Google Maps to show you how to get back home,
People used to talk face-to-face
Now without buttons they'd be in a daze,
Turning back the clock it was so much better
It's a forgotten art a hand-written letter,
Saturday's time for the Grand Ole Opry
Who can forget Minnie Pearl yelling "Howdy"?
Dinner on the ground and all the fixin's
Or Grandpa Jones and his banjo pickin',
String Bean's pants too short for a short man
One thing's for sure he sure could sing,
People back then generally sought after good
Close by the stove a coal bucket stood
With coal and pieces of wood,
Coil oil lamps to help light the night
Most fitting for my world with somber bright,
Don't remember dreading walking to school
Keep a sharp ear no surprises rule,
We buckled down and learned the three R's

No one I know loves a liar,
Friday afternoons playing under clear sky of blue
Teachers made work time fun too,
Sometimes we simply made up things to do
Other times it was welcomed to have a little solitude,
Our imagination was able to soar
Early to rise walking barefoot across the floor,
And all-wooden wagon was fun to make
Afternoons of pastime made.

Another winter set in
Flashed back to another time I've been,
Waking up early under a blanket of white
Tree limbs weighted from the sprinkled night,
As gleams of sunlight struck
Difficult sounds coming from a lone truck,
The snow sparked like a diamond ring
Where's food a lone bird would sing,
Putting aside the book I've read
Bread crumbs on the porch I'd spread.
Remembering under warm bed covers a night's dream
Out gathering snow for Mom to make snow cream,
Raking back the layer of snow sprinkled soot
Avoid all places of splashed under foot,
Mom always knew how to excite her kids
My path directed from the things she did,
Tracking signs of ole red's hoof
Avoid icicles hanging from the roof,
Oh thoughts in my head how they live on
Even though changes come they are not gone.

Winter's over spring has sprung
'Click and wheel' how they clang,
The budding of life and new beginnings
How wide the streams slowly receding,
Far blown fresh smells the air
Kids playing truth or dare,
Nature busy about renewing
A wondrous site divinely seeing,
The earth shakes off the last remnants of chill
Finally outside doing what we will,
Happy the sounds voices over a game of marbles
In the distance others playing a game of ball,
The girls off playing their games too
A dog chasing another it's true,
All life welcomed the warm sun
Too late to see that which a spider spun,
This renewed exhilarating life I'm in
Looking back through childhood eyes I've been,
Really seeing a flower how beautiful they are
Foreign it seems a car's wayward tire,
If I dream what does it leave
Hopes of joy of memory I believe,
Pictures are proof of the old days
Squirrel hunting through the morning haze,
How sweet the smell of nature's sense
Pause given thanks do you know from whence,
Life is a mystery so thin
Thanks be we know not when.

9/23/19

Christmas

Oh! Is this Christmas?
Every child will cheer
They'll receive gifts and make
New resolutions to the coming year.
Christmas captures our hearts
And imagination,
When we reflect we become spell bound by
Overwhelming tradition.
Looking back on my childhood times were
Hard and they were rough,
But we were rich with love who
Dare say we hadn't enough?
Through it all there were times we
Thought we lost each other,
Now remembering back it seemed
All we had was one another.
Christmas is a glorious time of sharing
And listening to the chimes,
When it's over all we have
Are the words of a rhyme adding it
To the other memories lost in time.

1992

We'll look back on our lives

Time and again,

We'll dance again,

We'll sing again,

We'll laugh again,

But

We'll never be young again.

1980

5

Looking Back: Family

Aunt Ethel

A little house nestled in front of a meadow
With a big barn in the back,
I watched you pick apples till you were tired
Then pile them on the porch from your grass sack.

Walking up the path the house came into view
I heard someone ask, "Is that you?"

The sweet smell in the air was coming from the house
I walked closer and I knew it was beans cooking in a kettle,
Walking in the yard I could see everyone
Some were playing, then I remembered,
And I asked, "Where is Ethel?"

1985

Climb, Brandon, Climb

It was early to be sweating
Securing the anchors deep,
Good shoes kept from slipping
Your body weight the rope did keep,
Surveying the crevices
Stay focused on the task ahead,
Carabiners only part of the devices
A must to be five moves ahead.

I was on the ground when you started
Gazing up through flashes of reflection,
Always prepared never half hearted
Your first love shown through your determination.
Still the rock was cold
As dust from the chalk bag flew,
It can't be done voices said you're too old
Traces of clouds speeding to blue.

Your name could be at the top
Too close now for mistakes,
If you make it and don't drop
Danger is always present something could break,
So high the contrast so vivid
Failure is not an option any longer,
I suddenly understood your free spirit
As a youngster always the urge to conquer.

2/29/20

Gloria, Gloria

Gloria, Gloria what can I say
        We stayed with you all night
And part of a day,
        We loved your home and your piano too
One luxury of being together
        We could sit around and think of things to do.

I wished we lived closer
        Then you could yell at us
For getting your house dirty,
        Maybe you'd get used to Brandon
Screaming in the night for food
        At twelve and again at five thirty.

But no matter where we're at
        We could have fun,
We could laugh and talk after breakfast
        And watch Bob getting the dishes done.

September ended and October began
        We had a great time
And we'll see you when we can.

1986

Sheila, Sheila

Through the early years there was a time
        It was just me, you, and Gloria,
The times I still adore
        The days seemed long and the nights in part,
The birthdays seemed to never arrive
        Though we wished them away in our hearts.

Through all the good and bad
        All the playful memories we had,
Through the years
        Now the years,
Have crept between us
        We no longer have the luxury to cuss or fuss.

I hope this birthday is as happy as the ones we shared
        Way back when,
As we keep score remember to savor it
        Cherish it,
Don't let time whisper it away in the wind
        We need to always take time,
So long has the time passed, the things we say and do
        This is my humble way to say "Happy Birthday"
To someone as special as you.

1988

CDWorley
3-30-21
Mom

Oh, MOM

Mom, I wept for you 21 years ago
Minute-by-minute, hour-by-hour it was so,
The day you left still seems like a dream
Mourning for you is not enough it seems,
A deep survey of your life might help me
It might leave me more to see,
Will it answer the questions I seek?
Oh, Mom, if we could have one more week.

In the past there's a looming question one more day
So overjoyed seeing you no time for anything to say,
Other family and friends would want to see
The day would go so fast no time for me,
As a girl on the farm you did the work of a young man
Becoming a young woman didn't matter, your dad saying
yes you can,
If one isn't enough what about day two?
Summers came and went growing fast survey since 1922
The farm came first plant and reap
Oh, Mom, if we could have one more week.

Mom, when your oldest brother left home
That must have made you feel all alone,
Stepping up you became the oldest
Without your consent you were the closest,
Extra energy spent your dad's temper showed through
Poor animals received his anger much better than you,
Hurting your feelings when he clamored
Grasped his fingers hitting the mule with his hammer,

Again I ask, could everything be squeezed into day three?
Your mind also would be racing with things you want to
free
The stars of night please let me sleep
Oh, Mom, if you and I had one more week.

Your dad tried teaching you the plow
Hard you tried weaker in body would not allow,
From freight to knowing could you ever please your dad
The nights flew, the mornings were always a dread,
The depression magnified the difficulties too
Mom, what were your dreams or did woe overtake you,
Consuming you must have been the thought of leaving
The thought of leaving your mom would be deep
sorrowing,
Throwing rocks at boys tried getting too close
The reluctant mule his pounding nostrils white with frost,
Remembering your love for talking so keen and more
Now would there be enough time in day four,
Would you again take a stroll in bare feet
Oh, Mom, if you and I had one more week.

Mom, you tried running the first time you saw him
What crossed your mind or was it the light dim,
The mules, the chickens, the piggies' squealing sounds
Dad won you over and you came around,
You married so young
You thought you'd be free and on your own,
It was different, marriage and farming, or more of the
same?
Then the day decided came
Did you ever hear the words I love you?
Did dad ever tell you?

Through all your toil and stress
With 7 kids you endured more hard work cleaning their
mess,
The morning I was born it's a miracle you survived
We'd just get started with day five,
Mom, you were a woman so strong and so unique
Oh, Mom, if you and I had one more week.

Mom, when you learned Dad was not the one
The hurt you must have felt like a storm without a rising
sun,
The rest of your life you searched but never found
Did you wish you were born in another time, another
town?
Your kids were the center of your life
Motherly love rose up the day I cut my finger with a knife,
Washing clothes with your hands building fires to warm
the house
A weaker woman would have disappeared like a mouse,
Did you regret you'd never reach your potential?
Although you were the rock of the family without
credentials,
The high standards you transferred to me
In your kids proof you lived for all to see,
Your inner struggles how you kept those hid
I never once thought you might not be there when I was a
kid,
Your red hair gave a brilliant contrast to any mix
I know no way there'd be enough time in day six,
As I grew I knew your love for dad was not deep
Oh, Mom, if I could have one more week.

It's not hard the question for seven is for me
It's also not hard an uncloudy sky is easy to see,
It's also selfish of me the words I never got to speak
Would the gain be worthy of awaking you from eternal
sleep?
Mom, I took it for granted you would always be
Never gave a thought a time without you and me,
The question isn't for arguing what would I do with the
time
The precious moments we spent then were mine,
So here I am with all these questions you see
But you would say, was not 77 years enough for you and
me?

Oh, Mom, your life was so hard
My feeble attempt to tell all on a card,
If it was easy I'd say what about day eleven
One, two, three, or four, five, six, and seven?
I never told you I loved you nearly enough
Was it because we, too, lived through times so rough,
It's not easy admitting my failures
A day turned to a week then a month now many years,
There's a pleasant path awaits me to your holy place
maybe a distant star
The shadows of a sunset looking through a window so far,
The hills and valleys of life and in the middle a quiet
stream
Mom, you raised a dreamer that dares to dream,
Beautiful trees and a colorful sky
In the distance rolling mountains so high,
From the stream small ones break off into ponds
If you concentrate lilies can be seen floating along the
banks and beyond,

The grass multiple colors of green sprinkled all through
with flowers
I can see you and me sitting for hours,
The aroma of sweet roses mixed with honeysuckle too
All this and more awaits me and you,
Angelic voices drawing nearer
My hopes in another place much greater,
I painted this picture in words to leap
Mom, I couldn't settle for one more week.

10/10/19

Sherdina, Sherdina

You're having another birthday
>   And you're feeling the worst,
And you think you have to
>   Drink, shout, and curse,
So this year do things a little different
>   Don't do the things you shouldn't,
I'd love you more if you wouldn't
>   Think of your years as,
The harmony in a song
>   It takes time,
Before the words will come along
>   Sometimes rhymes are sweeter than honey,
And you are special just like your name
>   The only thing about words it won't spend like money,
Wishing you a special day
>   Day in and day out you're always the same.

1986

Wanda, Wanda

We liked your furniture and your new painting
Really helped your décor look good,
    We got up to breakfast and ate the succulent dish
Your chef whipped up it was good food,
    We watched Leif and Kaiton play soccer
And trying to hit the target,
    I enjoyed going in your family room
And selecting an item from Kaiton's flea-market,
    Leif won his game
And Kaiton's team was beat,
    Later we took an hour
Trying to decide where to eat,
    On Sunday Mick was dressed sharp
And stepping high,
    When it came time to leave
I wished I didn't have to say good-bye,
    Wanda, Wanda what can I say
We stayed with you all night and all day.

Summer 1986

(I wrote this after visiting my sister Wanda
in Indianapolis. I think it was
one of our family reunions.)

Goodbye, Aunt Ethel

I know in more recent years
We haven't seen each other like we should,
And we haven't kept in touch
You know we could,
But time is the one thing
That will always remain,
Like the wind and the rain
There is one thing that will never change,
And will always be
Is the love between you and me.

1985

(I wrote this in a card and gave to my cousin Erma to read
to Aunt Ethel ... just days before she died.)

GDWorley
5/24/21
Carroll

Farewell, My Brother Carroll Lee Worley

(I wrote these thoughts after my brother died.
I had never been to a Catholic Funeral,
and I did not know if it would be open for anyone to speak.
If it had been, I would have shared these thoughts.)

Nine years and a few days between me and my brother Carroll Lee. Some of you may think to yourselves, how can someone stand before family and friends and speak at a time like this. Well to tell you the truth, I'm surprised myself. On the other hand, how can I not if given the opportunity to stand for someone I love. I've already had my time of crying and I'm sure there will be more. But after some time, this will transition to months of smiling and happiness, because I know where he's going.

So here I am standing before you like I'm strong and could go through and withstand anything. But when it counted the other day, when Madonna put the phone to Carroll's ear, and she told him it was me on the phone, I could barely hold back my emotion, and the only thing I was able to say was, "I love you," and I heard Carroll say, "I love you too."

At the time I was in my car driving. As the call came through, I'd pulled off the road just prior to that moment. I was thankful I did. Because it took several minutes to get ahold of myself. I began to think about why the only thing I was able to say was "I love you." I started trying to beat myself up, but after a while, it came to me at that moment, Carroll didn't need to hear a bunch of meaningless gibberish. We shared a moment and said to each other the most important thing we possibly could say. So moving forward

I have the memory we made Wednesday morning. His voice and what he said I'll never forget.

Over the past couple days, the difference in age between Carroll and myself would enter my thinking. At first, I brushed it off. I couldn't think of anything significant about the number 9, but it kept returning, and finally it dawned on me: 9 isn't significant unless you're the one nailed on a cross beside Jesus.

In the Bible, there was one man on each side of Jesus nailed on a cross. One of these men began to change when Jesus prayed for the crowd. This could have been when the man had a complete change of heart, and he spoke 9 words. (There's the number 9 again.) 9 words is very significant. It doesn't take a long-winded prayer to get the Lord's attention. 9 words, but it's a prayer of forgiveness. Lord remember me when you come into your kingdom. The man acknowledged Jesus as Lord, and where he was going, he wanted to be with him. Isn't that what we all want? It should be. I began to reflect on my life and so many memories I have with Carroll. 9 years doesn't seem like much unless you're 9 years old, and you have a brother that's 18 years old. When you're young, 9 years seems like a lifetime.

Even at that young age, Carroll had a fatherly instinct. So many times he would pull me aside and talk to me and give me advice on whatever I was going through. It could be something I was facing. I think he realized his role of being the older brother and how I looked up to him. Even though there are nine years difference in our age, he wasn't ashamed to be seen with me.

I remember going to a birthday party of one of my classmates when I was in grade school, and Carroll went with me. He didn't just take me and leave. He stayed the whole time and when it was over we walked home together.

When all is said and done, it's the memories we have left. My nephew William is in tune with realizing the importance of this. So many times he has said to me, let's make a memory today.

So I ask you what are you doing to make a memory? Every day we have the opportunity to touch someone's life in a positive way. Sometimes it might take words of encouragement or it might take a hug or sometimes holding someone's hand and saying nothing at all. All situations are different. How we react will determine if when we're gone, if others will remember the compassion we gave them.

How is your relationship with your children? My wife and I have gone through many difficult years with our son. There were times when I thought I would end up in the psych ward. Every day something reminded me don't give up, we're all he has between life and death.

Often times when I thought of my difficulties, I looked to my older brother. I was reminded of what he has gone through, my focus quickly shifted. Nineteen years ago God performed a miracle. Carroll was next to death. My sister Wanda remembers the doctor telling her and Carroll's immediate family his ejection fraction was 9 percent (a normal ejection fraction is 50 to 75 percent). Wanda at the time was staying with him daily and she changed the situation by having him transferred to the Ohio State University Heart Hospital and from there to Cleveland Clinic where upon arrival in a matter of hours, Carroll was in surgery and received a 39-year-old heart. Think about that, we had Carroll for 19 additional years. I also think that after his surgery, knowing the hand of God was upon his life, there was little doubt in my mind where he was headed after this life. To be absent from the body is to be present with the lord. That's what the Bible says.

Do you ever look up in the sky and think about where and how far away God resides? Well I do. God lives in the third heaven — you might ask where is the first and second heaven. Well, from earth to the edge of our atmosphere is the first heaven. Then from that point of leaving our atmosphere to all the solar systems that exist is the second heaven. At the end of the stars or 600 billion trillion miles starts the third heaven where God is. Bible scholars say it would take several hundred years to cover this distance with our earthly technology. Would you believe Carroll travelled this distance Thursday morning in 11 one hundreds of a second. The Bible says in a twinkling of an eye. A twinkle is blinking your eye. Well how fast can you blink?

No parent wants the misfortune of seeing their child die before they do. Mom and Dad had the good fortune of seeing him arrive in the arms of almighty God.

So let me close by saying this. To have a brother is one thing, to have a brother you can talk to and confide in about anything, I count that as being very fortunate. Because we don't choose our siblings. To have a friend is one thing. To have a friend that is as close to you as a brother, I count that as being very fortunate. Because we do choose who our friends are. To have both in one, I count this as being blessed. I stand before you today and can say in Carroll,

"I had both!"

10/4/14

Farewell, Mom

As I see everyone here today, Mom would love seeing all of you. She loved people. She loved people to come visit. When she was able, she loved to cook and wait on those around her. She made everyone feel welcome, and I can honestly say she not only made you feel welcome with her words but with action.

I remember her standing for hours cooking meals for relatives and friends and neighbors who came by just to visit. Anyone visiting Mom could not leave before eating a meal.

Mom was a seamstress, babysitter, and worked with children with disabilities, and while working with those children she learned sign language.

She loved reunions or a family gathering of any kind. She was the only person I ever knew that could carry on multiple conversations at the same time. I always wondered how she could do that. But that was Mom. Her mind was so sensitive, nothing got past her without notice.

Mom had the ability to teach and train me to be responsible, to be organized, to be respectful of others and their property without being obvious.

A disciplinarian she was — mom was about 5'1" with her shoes on. But as a boy growing up, if I'd been asked how tall is your mother, I would have said 10 feet tall. Disobedience she would not tolerate, and until this day I still wonder how she could swing a belt so fast.
She meant what she said, and I did exactly what she said.

The loving side of Mom was more dominant. I watched her cook meals on a stove that was fueled with wood and coal. As poor as we were growing up, I never missed a meal.

Most of the clothes we wore Mom made herself. I never went to bed dirty, and I always started the day with clean clothes. And she did this without running water in the house. The same clothes she spent hours making, she spent hours washing on a scrub board until a lot of times her fingers bled.

Mom taught her children how to be self-disciplined, and self-reliant. She taught my sisters how to be loving mothers.

Mom was always protective of her children. I remember when I was just beyond a toddler, Mom allowed me to walk to the grocery store, which was about ½ mile away with my sister Wanda. Everything was going fine until we started back home. The sun light dimmed; the clouds began turning black. Wanda began running for home at that moment. I didn't know why. She tried to make me run as fast as she did, but of course I couldn't. She ran on ahead and got safely home before this stuff began falling out of the sky. I never experienced that before. I managed to get to a little building about 50 yards away from home. There I was terrified, crying, and screaming for Mom; she came to me as fast as her legs would carry her, protected and hovered over me from what I later learned was rain. From that day throughout the rest of my life, I knew I could always count on Mom.

She seemed to have an inner strength to get her through any circumstance and come out on top. From that day until now there's been a lot of rainy days, but I learned from Mom how to get through them, and how to save for one when there's virtually little money coming in.

I want to say to Mom's brothers and sisters, how she adored each one of you. When she talked of you, it was always with kindness. I loved to hear Mom talk about her

being a little girl back on the farm, and how she respect-
ed her dad. She remembered some of the most humorous
things her brothers did as little boys — she cherished those
memories.

I think we can all find comfort in knowing she ac-
cepted the Lord as her savior.

About six years ago I began to see a change in Mom.
On several occasions she attended this very church we're
in today, with friends Laura Hicks and Laura Brown. She
commented to me how she loved to hear Brother Troxell
preach. It would thrill her so much after attending a ser-
vice.

When my brother Carroll underwent a heart trans-
plant, I truly believe this was Mom's wake-up call. I believe
God will shake a person's consciousness to the point of
where they are in relation to him. For Mom, she saw that
death is one heartbeat away, and life is regenerated with
your next breath, There's a fine line between the two. The
paths we choose after God places those roadblocks in our
lives determine where we will spend eternity. As Mom
became too ill to attend church, she devoted her time to
reading her Bible. Every time she read the Bible through,
she'd tell me, and I can remember four times. Regularly we
would have long conversations about the questions and
concerns she had. I would express my opinion — she'd tell
me hers. Then she would study and search it out for her-
self. That was encouraging to me, because that's what we're
supposed to do, and that is renewing our minds.

I have to ask the question I know some of you are
thinking. How can I stand before you and talk with the
passing of Mother. To answer that, I have to look at Mary
standing at the feet of Jesus hanging on the cross. I'm a son
who saw the pain and passing of Mother. Mary was the

mother who saw the pain and dying of her son. She saw him walking through the streets carrying a cross, bleeding, bruised, the crown of thorns on his head. Blood running down his face, being hit, spit on, and despised. She saw him walk up the hill of Golgotha, demoralized and weak, thrown on the ground, watched those soldiers drive those Roman spikes into his hands and his feet. She saw the hurt in his eyes when that cross dropped into its final resting place, seeing the blood and agony, the human side of Mary's emotion had overwhelmed her. This was her son — once she held in her arms as a baby and watched him grow into a man.

Now Jesus did something miraculous not long before he was to take his last breath — he saw the hurt in his mother's eyes. Jesus knew his mother's emotions had flooded her mind. He had to wake her up to the fact of who he is. I believe this because of what he said: "Mother, behold thy son." I believe as weak as Jesus was at that moment, those words came through loud and clear. Mother, don't look at this human body in all its frailties. Mother, remember the Holy Spirit inside you causing conception in her womb, and the word became flesh and dwelt among us. He also was telling the disciple standing next to Mary, she is now his mother and, without saying it, someone to take care of from this point on.

Mother, behold thy son. The Lord had to draw her mind to the spiritual place of where he wanted her to be and to give her a purpose.

Mother, behold thy son, The Lord was telling her, the disciple standing next to you is for you to take care of.

Today I'm saying this to you in the reverse, behold my mother, her spirit is in the hands of a just God. The word says it's appointed unto man once to die and after that the judgement. One day after a while Mom will pick up this body again, just as Christ picked up his earthly body when he was resurrected.

In first Corinthians, Chapter 15, we are born the image of the earthy. We shall also bear the image of the Heavenly. We shall all be changed in a moment, in the twinkling of an eye.

We shall all be changed!

I love you, Mom!

1998

(I wrote this 10-12 hours before funeral service and did speak at Mom's service.)

I'm like a rainbow, I come up when the

Storm's over.

7/9/19

6

Looking Back: A Sundry Collection

Work in Progress

Stepping into the elevator for the half mile ride down,
You have the usual momentary qualms in your belly
And a bursting sensation in your ears,
Getting near the bottom when the drop slows so abruptly,
You swear it is going upward again as your
Eyes water with tears.

When the doors open, your eyes are forced shut
Feeling the initial fierce blasts of air,
The ventilation system sucking air out as the huge
Fans are forcing air back in,
The heavy smell of gases, sulfur, and dust
Are so familiar it's barely noticeable,
The taste of coal creeps in one's mouth
That's why talking is not advisable.

The weak feeling in your legs is not recognized
Until bending over,
Crawling on hands and knees through a small
Passageway, he is overwhelmed with stress,
No way around dust and water before
Getting to the room to work,
Sprawling in the muck for a minute to catch
Your breath, before you can be a work in progress.

1973

The Future

In choosing a profession for the future
Is sometimes difficult,
One must be sure he will be happy
Working in that particular area.

I have chosen art as my career
The enjoyment I get from working in art,
Started at a very early age
But not until three years ago,
Did I decide to become a professional artist?

The advantages of art
Can hardly be explained in words,
Art has helped me to see myself
And my environment more clearly,
Also art has helped me to know
Real beauty isn't looking at someone,
But beauty is seeing that person
And beyond the face.

Imagination is a necessity
To become successful in art,
For example, observing an ancient ruins
Or a deserted house,
I'm able to use all my senses just by seeing.
By seeing a child's work of art,
I can better understand him
And how far his mind has developed,
In relation to his age.

By becoming an artist
I can better understand people,
And help them better understand themselves
And their environment.

1974

Regret

As I enter the evening of life I look back
It's true some will hurt you can bet,
Although some pieces seem to, but don't really attack
I hope I should be the only one with regret.

Putting away childish things doesn't mean I don't
remember
Those I had the good fortune to meet my life was touched,
Enjoying an evening and smelling the last remains suppers'
embers
The places and mountains and faces and such.

They are no longer where I remember to see
Many are now gone to eternal sleep,
My early days life and work is all I could see
Seemingly important things always in front of me.

My melancholy thoughts I need to let lie
Streams of honeysuckle carved around stone beneath my
breath,
Now all I have is life beneath the sky
The struggle of life was always in my path.

No one should have to go through this pain I'm feeling
The hurt in my spirit I must let it rest,
Forgiving oneself is harder than forgiven
My pendulous thoughts for days have overtaken my best.

Some people I know bundle those thoughts and suppress
I desperately want to go back and correct,
Daily I'm bombarded with this added stress
It swells in my sphere of regret.

Yes I can number all those faces in my head
I wish I could go back and the total of them I've beset,
Realizing the impossibility I excuse my guilt before I lay on
my bed
I hope I'm the only one that's carried regret.

8/13/19

Wanda, I Love You

Happy times you gave us all
Like happy days in spring,
Joyous moments you gave us all
That only a host like you could bring.

Bright seemed the morning on our second Christmas Day
The air sparkled with the words up, up, and away,
Let us not forget the food, its taste we remember
Glistening the air the wonder we ponder to the tune we
surrender.

Special thanks for the champagne, the words
I could not express when I was with you,
Hills and fields are forever, so are the words
I love you.

1981

(I wrote these thoughts after returning from a Christmas
family reunion held in Indianapolis. Wanda, my sister,
gave me and my wife a champagne toast for our upcoming
wedding anniversary.)

I'm like a butterfly, every day I wake

Up in a new world.

1/8/18

7

Words of Love

Magazine

Month after month
You came to me,
I sat quietly reading
Is this real you might have said to me.

I can see deep in your eyes
All you do is smile and the picture sales,
If a picture could talk
It's so hard to tell.

You captured me
I'm under your spell,
Then why do I feel forsaken
In this place I dwell.

I know this isn't normal
Your image can't set me free,
You can't stop me, I won't wait, I have to know if it's real
Or maybe I should be satisfied just paying the fee.

Once you told me it can never be
And I'll never learn,
I looked at your picture as I read
And another page is turned.

I called you on the phone
But a surrogate said no she doesn't know you,
It was a bad time
And you had things to do.

You can't imagine what your
Image means to me,
The magazine comes alive
Pacing the floor your eyes would follow me.

Your studio door read my image breeds
To everyone that reads but I wasn't diverted,
Work stopped as I forced my way free
Into your room, your help had been alerted.

Silence swept the room
As she stared at me for all to see,
I felt awkward and started to leave, "Wait," she said
She remembered our childhood, as I turned
She unfolded a picture of me.

1984

Gloria's Wedding Invitation

The news is out
So don't be late.
Come see Gloria and Bob
On the shown date.
They'll pledge their love
To each other.
You'll hear the words
They've already said to each other.
What a glorious time this will be
When Gloria and Bob
Say "I do" before you and me.
Don't miss this joyous time
And Celebration.
Isn't this a wonderful
Invitation?

1981

(Gloria, my sister, asked me to write her
Wedding invitation.)

The Meaning of Love

Love never dies of
A natural death,

It only dies when we forget
To seek others' highest good.

1998

How Does Love Die?

Love dies because we don't
    Know how to replenish its source.

It dies of blindness
    And errors and betrayals.

It dies of illness and wounds
    And weariness and withering.

It doesn't tarnish like something physical,
    It dies as we become so busy
    With life's trials.

So many to choose
    Leads us off course.

1998

The Power of Love

One true friend for someone
Fortunate it's more valuable than
Anything one might own.

Any single flower for someone
That truly looks,
Can bring as much joy as
A full bouquet.

If both should come one's way
Love crushes negativity away,
Equally a true friend causes one to rise above
Hate and fear can't stand next to the power of love.

5/25/20

Losing a True Love

One cold dark night
I was visited by a once true love,
In my lonely dark house
I could hear the softness of her voice,
I could feel her warm touch
And her eyes glowing, staring much,
It was so real I saw the door ajar
As I heard her knock,
I opened the door and she was standing there
In a flash I found myself alone with my hand in my hair,
I found myself staring into emptiness
I went back to bed,
Trying hard to forget the loneliness
I must try to forget her for a while,
Her spirit will come again
I never know when
Like the wind blowing wild.

1974

It is better to think

Of a way to forgive

Than to give vengeance

The Power of not letting you forget.

1984

8

Reflections on Religion

Rebirth

I could not have been happy in those days
Before I turned twenty-four,
Nor had the night considered the stars
Or counted the grains of sand on the shore.

I swear to you the God of heaven
God swore to God, for none was greater to swear,
He swears to us by the heavens, the heavens turn night into
day
Acknowledged his witness promises made,
In a walkway saturated with blood
Who passed away?

A daffodil is more arrayed than past kingdoms
In all their glory,
I am of more value than many sparrows
And I being talented have not hid my face from my master,
I am raised up a king
Loving kindness and tender mercies is my crown.

I believe I gained a lord
His supply is good things,
So that my youth is renewed like the eagles
What is grace?

1995

The First Day

The first day from eternity past
Could anyone go back and count?
Is it hard, have you seen, if I ask
Would the number be relevant?

Is my question hard, have you seen the first day?
Some say it's not the number but what you see,
What about the heat, some may say,
What about the buildings, cars, or city streets?

My question is simple, let's start again
It's the whole peeling back the layers,
The surface is not everything but everything therein
Anyone can see if they try leaving out the clever.

Let me explain
When the mist of moisture touches the surface,
The image in a mirror is darkly
As fresh air rushes in and cuts the haze,
The image becomes clearly.

Now it's plain
In the early morning the mist of fog has fallen,
The miracle of the eternal's handy work is overshadowed
The sun cuts through like a sweet voice calling,
Slothfulness is not the way
Many can see it
                    For some it's hard to see
                                        The first day.

8/12/14

The Son

A donkey led the caravan
Palm leaves follow falling from their hands,
        Reality runs on Jesus Christ
Our life he holds in his hands,
        Lord Jesus, you're all I ever needed
You're the one,
        His life to give, but
Resurrection was God's plan,
        Like freedom feels
When forgiveness comes,
        When faith collides,
When the earth was born,
        Light cometh from the Son.

2/1/18

Maybe It's Time

When I was young
    I felt the power of the universe leave me.
I was alone and what could I do?
    As I grew, I heard of a man called Jesus
The war was a battleground inside me,
    I didn't know how to stop it
I was afraid,
    I didn't know I was blind
And I could not see,
    One night a preacher said how to receive
All I had to do was believe.

Maybe it's time
    To give yourself to the one,
He'll give you purpose
    Placed in the body of the Son,
Maybe it's time
    To find your place in the sand,
The word became a man
    I asked the Holy Spirit to move in,
Dancing in the dark
    The stars were in tune with heaven's song,
    On the night, on the night
        You were reborn.

Yes, it's time
     You were the perfect lamb to be,
Only you, only you, you forgave me
     I looked up,
     Resurrection power gave me a new start
Dropping to my knees,
     I gave up the secrets of my heart
I found a love
     A home all my own,
He took my place
     Where I should have been,
His blood forever
     Covers my sin.

Maybe it's time
     To stop the struggle within,
     The majesty of the universe calling me
Dancing in the dark,
     The stars brightly dancing
The heavens singing in awe wondering,
     Yes, it's time
     He took my place,
     Where I should have been
His blood forever,
     Covers my sin
You were the perfect one,
Only you, your blood covers my sin
          Only you forgave me.

1/7/18

Why I Love You

If you've looked on a spring day
    And can't see,
Or you can't put together the reason
    As you see the sky above,
Can you see through the mist after a warm
    Rain ever so softly
Through the lens of nature and can't see love?

Have you asked why the sun
    Shines its radiant beam?
Or the beauty of a sunset the only
    Word comes out is "Awe."
Can you explain the wonder of looking
    At the stars and dream?
The only answer that can be said
    Is love.

The world would be a dreary
    Place without it,
Or the renewed feeling of waking up
    At dawn and know it comes from above,
Without love the forest would be cold
    Brittle, breaking, and split,
The eyes of man would be sad and
    Hopeless without love,
Without life-given sun rushing away the dawn
Or where would happiness be if it was gone?

And I know the creator loves me
    The purpose of my existing is to love him back,
And the sunshine he gives me
    With the joy it brings,
But I know love exists even though
    The sky is blue
Makes me know why I love you.

2/17/21

Glorious

Lord, thank you for forgiveness
Many times I got off track,
All the wrongs I've committed
And unseemly acts.

You were there with outstretched arms.

Many times I could have given more than I would
Instead of placing blame, touched every life I could,
When I said no to you and willingly went out on my own
Not realizing others would hurt,
The real trouble and heartaches will follow the life I've
sewn.

You were always standing near.

When others are hungry and food is scarce,
When their stomachs are full, then we can point them to
the cross.
Don't allow the mistakes of the past repeat in your future
Decisions we think are right some become regrets,
When we apply the truth before our departure.

Lord, thank you for letting me take this journey
This thing we call life on this earth,
If given a choice I could not have picked
A better family at my birth.

In your word all we know about heaven
Is that it's glorious,
Many times I wondered
As I read and pondered,
The answer was right before me
I could not handle a description more tremendous,
Stupendous, miraculous, or even fabulous
Lord, just let me see Glorious.

2/2/18

The First Drop

We were like children when they took him away
Awakened from dreams seem broken,
We were all there but couldn't make it go away
Somebody kissed him, that's the one to be taken.

The news from within they're beating him somebody said.
Who's defending him? Now all hope seems lost.
Hope, joy, and peace still swirling in my head
All but one ran hiding and then I saw the cross.

What happened to love?
What happened to the word? It all came crashing in.
It was the sweetest sound
When the first drop of blood hit the ground.

Then the eyes of Jesus I could clearly see
Brighter than any star as they fell on me,
Staring, his mother and me, as darkness filled the land
His body covered as the blood kept coming down,
The ground tried to disappear it was the loudest sound
When the first drop of blood hit the ground, hit the ground,
The first drop hit the ground.

I walked with you for three years barefoot in the sand
You proved who you were,
The word made flesh and grew into a man
The light pushed back the dark as it came back around,
I began asking myself his love I had found
The blood was steady now,
As the drops kept hitting the ground.

Then the eyes of Jesus I could clearly see
Brighter than any star as they fell on me.
He looked at his mother and said behold thy son
He looked at me and said behold thy mother.
I knew what he meant, she's now my mother it was clear to
me
I would take care of her as in the days to come he will take
care of me.

He gave me a purpose and I knew where I stood
His body completely covered now, the blood kept coming
down.
The drops were steady. It was the loudest sound.
As his drops of blood hitting the ground
Hit the ground,
When the first drop hit the ground.

Thinking strength had left my legs and I could not move
The image I was seeing tears flooded my eyes.
Jesus promised life after this and the gift of love
I knew somehow the Devil was behind this with his pack
of lies.
We held on to each other trying to catch our breath
My strength, mother would need me now as we both saw
his head droop down.

Then the eyes of Jesus I could clearly see
Brighter than any star as they fell on me,
Staring, mother and me, as darkness filled the land
His body covered as the blood kept coming down.
The ground tried to disappear
It was the loudest sound.

When the first drop of blood hit the ground
Hit the ground,
The first drop hit the ground.

1/4/18

9

Denouement

Falling Star

In the limpid expanse of time
With reflecting colors struggling for mobility and forming,
Began the sixth morning.

A just born trembling earth evoked a structure
With volcanic molten odors,
The sun was hazy crimson shinning on the clovers
Soon an animal would appear with only leaves for covers.

Within the earth's particular dimension
On her barely perceivable bi-distinct forms
Has finally settled,
Little did her contours know
It would be the testing ground for a great battle.

Something between a bone and nothing
Ignorance and intelligence,
Something between the dirt and a glimpse from heaven
The spirit within the animal destined to
Rule the world,
Man appeared.

Slowly raising himself up looking at the sky
Breathtaking beauty his mind had to comprehend splendor
on,
Such grandeur moments before had not seen through his
eyes.

At that very instant the celestial bodies' atmosphere was
magnificent
Gases of reflecting colors so bright
From one to all the stars.

The eternal with his approval of everything now visible
All is good within his vision so bright across the sky
Man called it a falling star.

1976

Also published by Charles Dan Worley

Coming Soon From

Charles Dan Worley ...

- Co-op, Part 2
- A Western Novel